… IN INTERIORS

'We believe that the aesthetics of interior design are shaped by lighting.'
I IN

CONTENTS

009	FOREWORD
010	INTRODUCTION What Do You See?

PROJECTS

014	CARTIER GUEST LOUNGE
032	POKÉMON CENTER OKINAWA
050	YA-MAN
066	THELIFE
084	CARTIER JAPAN OFFICE
102	MASTERMIND
118	MARUNOUCHI HOUSE TOILET

134	INTERVIEW

PROJECTS

140	BLUE BOTTLE COFFEE UMEDA CHAYAMACHI CAFÉ
158	PINOCCHIO
174	WARP STUDIO
192	SHISEIDO FUTURE SOLUTION LX
208	GOODLIFE
226	LULLA HOUSE

247	AFTERWORD
248	PROJECT INFORMATION
249	SPECIAL THANKS

FOREWORD

As we adapt to the digital era, the role of designers is to constantly reassess our physical spaces. The digital revolution has altered our interaction with interiors. This shift has led to the emergence of reverse skeuomorphic design, where physical design is inspired by digital elements. It has also redefined familiar concepts. For instance, the meaning of luxury has evolved in this new age. The function of materiality and the role of experiences have become crucial aspects of design. Designers are now tasked with effectively crafting these experiences.

I IN, a Tokyo-based design studio, explores these questions through its work. Striking a balance between innovation and simplicity, it aims to redefine the conventional Japanese design studio. This transformation, while radical, remains respectful of traditional values and Japan's rich design heritage.

Honouring its cultural heritage, I IN is challenging the norms of the Japanese design industry. It aims to transform the traditional model of design studios in Japan, typically led by a single prominent designer. Instead, I IN operates as a collaborative endeavour under the leadership of its principals, Yohei Terui and Hiromu Yuyama.

I IN thrives on collaboration. Based on mutual challenge and respect, this approach propels the studio and fosters innovation. While collaboration may extend project timelines and necessitate compromise, I IN values its transformative potential. Over time, the principals have developed a deep understanding, harmoniously balancing shared values and creative tension in their work. This dynamic partnership is a unique asset, distinguishing I IN in the Japanese design landscape.

The definition of luxury has evolved significantly in our modern age, adapting to changing consumer values and technological advancements. Today, luxury is less about material rarity or social status and more about sensory experiences. Industrialisation has made many once-coveted items widely accessible, shifting the perception of luxury. In a world where most structures are built economically for basic functionality and profit, thoughtful and intentional design has become a new form of luxury. A luxurious space now evokes emotion and engages all five senses. This is achieved not through traditional material extravagances but through a space's immaterial and sometimes fleeting aspects. It's about the quality of sound, the perception of light, and the impact of scent. In essence, luxury has shifted from being about 'what' space is to 'how' it is experienced.

In the pages ahead, readers will find simply yet thoughtfully designed interiors, each featuring at least one innovative element that redefines spatial design. The projects, captured in high-quality photographs, embody the new luxury I IN promotes. The commentary provides insight into I IN's practices and methods, further elaborated in the interview section. This offers an introduction to a unique type of Japanese design studio – one that challenges established norms while respecting its heritage.

Noor Al Qayem
and François-Luc Giraldeau

INTRODUCTION
- What Do You See? -

Many architects and designers settle for a signature look very early in the game. Or, at the very least, they strive for one – a visual DNA that semaphores the world precisely, which is the creative mind behind a particular design. It's a useful calling card, especially as it helps the studio stand out from the pack for its distinctive house style. For I-IN and its founders, Hiromu Yuyama and Yohei Terui, no obviously distinctive markers in their work might lead the observer to instantly say of a built space, 'Ah, yes, that's work by I IN. It's unmistakable.'

If there is a signature look, it is contained less in actual physical cues than in an attitude. A quiet thoughtfulness that underpins any one of their designs. A mature coherency of thought. A disciplined line of reasoning that runs through the entire project. Still, for all the elusiveness, there are some discreet clues if you know where to look. Often, it's in the way lighting is harnessed to evoke an emotional resonance in the space. Sometimes, it's in the materiality of furnishings and fittings. And just as often, it's how a space is resolved. Such as the floor plan for the Pokémon Center, where the space morphs according to the nature of the products on display, a sleight of hand created by exploratory paths that are as complex as wandering around in a cave, even though the space actually comprises only two concentric circles.

To encounter an I IN project is to engage at least one, if not all, of the five human senses. Emotional. Sensorial. Auditory. Tactile. In the case of Terui and Yuyama's first project, a bijou bakery in Yokohama, it was olfactory. In fact, for a debut, the modest space shows remarkable maturity in the way simple, hard-working materials are harnessed to impart a simultaneously sophisticated, modern and nostalgic quality. Linger a little in each of I IN's spaces – touching a surface here, sitting quietly in a room there, watching how someone else moves through the space elsewhere – and something shifts internally. A recognition of an emotional heft that bears all the hallmarks of a frisson of je ne sais quoi. 'If we prioritise designs that can be explained in words,' they say, 'we will have to give up designs that cannot be explained in words.' Heaven forbid.

For a designer to feel and approach design this way is unusual enough. To find two, much less two working together in the same studio is that rare moment when lightning is captured in a bottle. Even more remarkable is that Terui and Yuyama both began their careers in Curiosity, the revered design studio of Gwenael Nicolas, where the sum of their individual characters, life interests and approach to design began to shape and temper their nascent sense of space, proportions and colours. It didn't take them long to realise the value of searching for new expressions no one had ever seen. Dreaming up ideas with no preconceptions and then repeatedly experimenting and refining – a process blending attitude and mindset that continues to form the touchstone of I IN's work.

To hear Yuyama tell it, their time at Curiosity was marked with design aphorisms that bordered on being koans. 'One of the most memorable things Gwenael said to me was, "Don't design a device that drops water. Instead, design the landscape created when water drops fall on the water's surface." That means if you design something caught up in shape and colour, it will not be a design that resonates with people. This is why we always want to create designs that move people.' On every metric, I IN – formally instituted by Terui and Yuyama on 8 January 2018 – is a meeting of minds, a congenial harmonisation of two histories, two perspectives and two minds into a shared approach to design. There is a certain bravado in their output, but one that is anchored in faith in their capabilities and a certainty that if their designs are good enough, people will respond and even doubters will eventually come around.

At I IN, the pair are unapologetic about their work. Not out of hubris and mind but from an understanding that good design based on conviction and sound fundamentals will eventually stand the test of time. 'We may have no fixed, specific form, but we do believe in the purpose of our designs,' they say. 'And we believe that purpose is to open the door for people to receive our ideas. Therefore, we always avoid working with the same people or materials. Yes, it's a little scary not knowing how things will turn out, but we believe that expanding our world seeds new ideas and design.'

Ideas such as how light is integrated into a space. How can design be rendered humanistic and connected to the natural environment through landscapes, materials and light? Terui remembers Jennifer Stearns, his mentor at Parsons School of Design, who drummed into him the idea that creating interior spaces is not just about the surface but includes the composition of volumes and the lighting rhythm. 'She taught me that lighting can be a sublime beauty.' The experiential quality of a space is also important. When you see a space from the outside, how does that prepare you for the experience you will have when walking five steps inside? What kind of space, what kind of experience awaits you?

Yuyama remembers the first time he walked into Shigeru Ban's Nomadic Museum, a vast conceptual exhibition space that toyed with the visitor's sense of light and sound. 'I had such a "Wow!" moment when I walked in. But a sense of comfort also made me want to stay forever.' Of course, as easy as it may be to articulate these theoretical musings, the challenge comes in translating them into reality and useable spaces. As the following pages demonstrate quite clearly, this philosophy of simplifying the centre of gravity of a space as much as possible so that an immersive, discursive quality emerges surfaces in project after project.

You see it in the use of binary colours and light to permeate – no, saturate – the public toilets at Marunouchi House. The quotidian washroom experience is transformed into something memorable in one fell swoop. In the offices and guest lounge of Cartier, the sensation of being inside a lush red and gold lined jewellery box is unexpected, subliminally arch, luxurious and humorous at the same time. To collectively scan I IN's projects in this way, one after the other, is to be struck by three correlated points. The first is Diana Vreeland's axiom, which states that the eye must travel. The second is to come to terms with how far the studio has come quickly. And the third – just how mysterious is the creative process.

For in the world, according to Terui and Yuyama – by any yardstick, the confident voices of a new generation of Japanese slash global designers – the genesis of creation is as ineffable as the finished product. And to an extent, any attempt to analyse the individual parts that eventually make up the whole is Sisyphean in its futility. All that matters is the human response. Only when all the different aspects of a design are aggregated and become a single design, say Terui and Yuyama, will the observer be able to relate and respond and say, 'I see.'

Daven Wu,
Singapore Editor, Wallpaper*

PROJECTS

CARTIER GUEST LOUNGE

OFFICE
TOKYO, JAPAN (2022)

The Guest Lounge at Cartier Japan brings the elegance and virtues of the prestigious luxury brand to the work environment. Above all, it provides guests with a sublime, memorable spatial experience. Ambient lighting from the ceiling bathes the entire lounge, softening the gentle forms of the interiors. The homogenous lighting uses the space like natural daylight, creating a visually unique floating sensation that is uplifting and inspiring. A grand counter stands at the centre, its majestic presence forming the axis of the entire space and drawing the focus to the quality of its custom-made materials. Beneath, the delicate patterns of wood grain radiate outward across the floor, defining the counter space, which is enveloped by the surrounding lounge area. Large plush sofas line the walls, their colourful cushions creating a warm visual rhythm. With luxurious lighting, these elements float weightlessly in the space. The Maison's creativity is expressed throughout the spatial design through meticulously chosen shapes, forms, combinations of materials and ambient lighting. It's a lounge space of bold elegance that gives its guests a luxury experience.

POKÉMON CENTER OKINAWA

RETAIL
OKINAWA, JAPAN (2022)

The Pokémon Center is a hub of all things Pokémon – a store, gaming space and information centre to share the latest character and game news. Inspired by the worldview of the Pokémon franchise, the Pokémon Center is designed to give visitors the impression of stepping into a video game. Its open-plan circular enclosure and continuous floor space resemble architectures of an imaginary world while evoking the caverns and landscape of the Pokémon universe. The Monster Ball, its iconic shiny red and blue case, is repeatedly referenced throughout the space but in minimalist graphic forms. This balance of design subliminally shifts the focus from the space to the understanding of Pokémon that develops within the space. Abstract and bold representations of Okinawa's abundant nature, ocean waters and verdant greenery add to the otherworldly space's immersive nature. Colour and texture evoke deep waters at the circular core and heart of the Pokémon Center, where visitors can access information and Pokémon games through videos and presentations. Surrounding this lie experience zones with changing content to continuously excite visitors – spaces that introduce card games, showcase new visual media and offer the latest goods. The Pokémon universe is already well known to the public; however, this physical store can convey the appeal of Pokémon to an even wider audience by connecting the virtual and real worlds.

©2022 Pokémon. ©1995-2022 Nintendo/Creatures Inc./GAME FREAK inc.

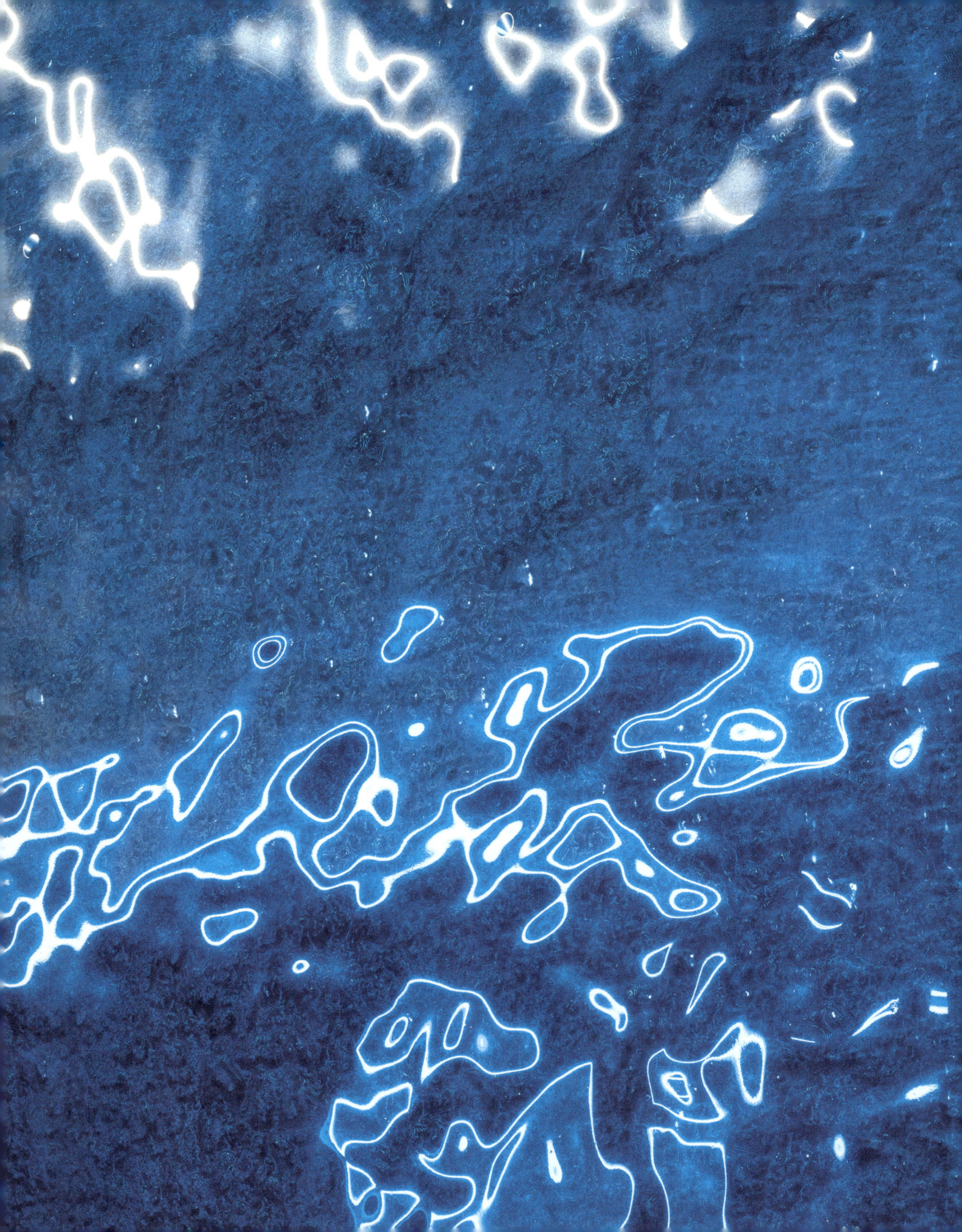

©2022 Pokémon. ©1995-2022 Nintendo/Creatures Inc./GAME FREAK inc.

042

©2022 Pokémon. ©1995-2022 Nintendo/Creatures Inc./GAME FREAK inc.

©2022 Pokémon. ©1995-2022 Nintendo/Creatures Inc./GAME FREAK inc.

©2022 Pokémon. ©1995-2022 Nintendo/Creatures Inc./GAME FREAK inc.

YA-MAN

RETAIL
TOKYO, JAPAN (2024)

The global flagship store design for YA-MAN, a beauty equipment brand that utilises technology to elevate beauty. The store is divided into two floors; on the first floor, products are displayed for purchase, while the second floor serves as the FACE LIFT GYM section – a training facility specialising in facial muscle training using their products. The main design aim of this store was to create a new, luxurious environment, offering a distinctive beauty experience for all beauty seekers. The impactful presence of the YA-MAN store is magnified along Ginza's Chuo-Dori Avenue, characterised by its expansive horizontal façade, with luminous design elements radiating outwards onto the street. Upon entering the first floor, guests are greeted by a magnificent wall of light inspired by the concept of their facial beauty device, in which LED light is an integral part of their technology. This captivating feature is showcased in an ample booth space where visitors are bathed in light, offering an unforgettable experience. The colour of the light wall changes, with its spectrum determined by incorporating the wavelength of the LED used in their products. In addition, the point light source is diffused in multiple directions, penetrating deeply into the viewers through a glass specially processed to resemble human skin cells. The display areas are lit up individually within the overall space composed of subdued tones, where the interplay of light and dark creates a pleasant rhythm, giving the impression of products gracefully floating in the air. Gold accents are applied to various parts of the display area to enhance the luxurious experience of the product and its space. Technology and luxury are fused together in this store design. The second floor is where the FACE LIFT GYM is located, where natural light permeates each corner, creating a leisurely passage of time. The entire floor is made up of a series of open treatment booths that offer a moderate degree of privacy, curating a collection of individual experiences. Inspired by the products, soft light lines are rhythmically placed above each booth, forming an accent recognisable from the outside. At the back of the building lies a cavernous VIP room, providing an even more refined experience where guests are immersed in a luxurious space of deep white and gold. An extraordinary light experience is crafted to showcase YA-MAN's beauty world from Japan to the rest of the world.

FA

THELIFE

RESIDENCE
TOKYO, JAPAN (2021)

The residence apartment is 40 years old and located in Shibuya, Tokyo. Opening the door, the volume of abstract natural light welcomes you, giving you a sense of the atmosphere of the room behind. The experience of each space, such as the entrance, the corridor and the entrance hall, leads to a private area by slowly revealing the layers of the space. In the entrance hall, a flower piece is draped on the wooden door with a strong presence, and a bench made out of solid wood extracted from a single cherry tree stands in the warm light. The material expression allows you to feel the solidity and depth, and the details that create a soft and light impression influence each other to realise a sophisticated and luxurious space. The indirect lighting surrounding the entire room and the ceiling light beam above the kitchen counter, emitted from the shape of the room itself, eliminates the existence of the lighting source and creates a space where only pure light exists. By openly connecting the rooms, the whole space is illuminated by spreading the lighting throughout its surface. The bright nuance of the flooring and the delicate texture of the oak on the wall capture the rich light that flows throughout the space. The walk-in closet, wrapped in wood, has lighting integrated with each storage. The metal's texture, contrasted with the wood, reacts to light and creates a high-quality, fresh impression. I IN proposes a new way of living in a residential space with unprecedented sophistication and luxury.

CARTIER
JAPAN OFFICE

OFFICE
TOKYO, JAPAN (2022)

The Cartier Office renovation design aims to express the prestigious brand's world view of creativity, excellence and luxurious experiences by using experiential spaces to foster new communication and relationships within the work environment. A brightly lit and airy entrance hall with high-quality materials sets an uplifting mood in the office. Original abstract artwork of scattered gold leaf on the wall next to the entrance welcomes guests with a contemporary, majestic flair. The staff locker room offers a space of tranquillity, its tone subdued in contrast to its surroundings, while within the office spaces, accents of champagne gold and deep red are tempered by natural hues – subtle references to the luxury of artisanal craft. A circular lounge space, enclosed within soft-sheen vertical louvres, brings a sense of calm and comfort, its privacy heightened by mellow lighting from above and red-coloured sofas that wrap around its visitors. Carefully selected materials and innovative lighting enhance the open-plan work and communication areas. A central large round table has a radial wooden surface pattern, subtly divided into individual work zones by champagne-gold metal lines. The communication lounge, radiantly lit by its window-side location, offers spaces that encourage face-to-face encounters and conversations. A marble-topped circular counter welcomes visitors with its warm gold accents and open centre, while in a window-wrapped corner, a comfy plush sofa faces spectacular city views. Tucked in another window-walled corner lies the serene heart of the communication lounge. A raised tatami-mat space with unusual red mats looks out to vistas of the city. A space to take off your shoes to relax, stretch and decompress, it pays homage to Japanese aesthetics and honours Cartier's principles of artisanal quality and innovation.

MASTERMIND

OFFICE
TOKYO, JAPAN (2019)

Inspired by the minimalistic brand's philosophy, I IN designed a space with minimal elements emphasised by monochrome colour and light. Two identical layouts on two floors outline the workspace and the presentation areas. Each entrance with a contrasting space creates a different feeling between the front and back of the rooms, representing the character of each working space. Other lighting designs for each floor allow for an effect like a three-dimensional composition of lines enhancing the textured surfaces of the jet-black wood distributed throughout the space.

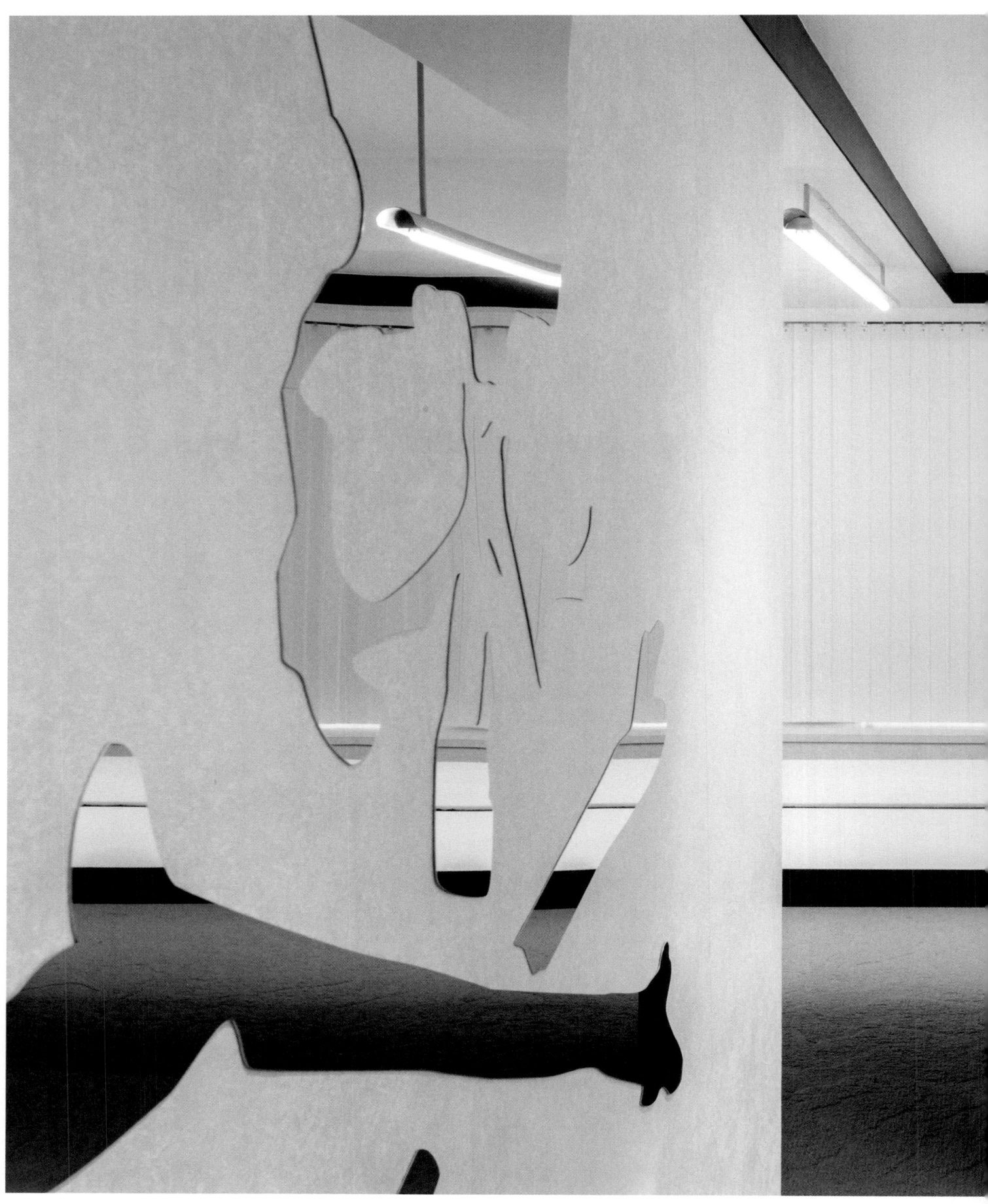

MARUNOUCHI HOUSE TOILET

PUBLIC TOILET
TOKYO, JAPAN (2023)

This public restroom of the (marunouchi) HOUSE restaurant floor of the Shin-Marunouchi Building proposes an innovative use of colour to blur the boundaries between gender. Yellow and green, two central and adjacent colours of the rainbow, are symbols of gender diversity and soften the gender divide long associated with conventional codes of red and blue. Inside, coloured light permeates the spaces, allowing visitors to experience the hues with their entire bodies. White tiling throughout – across floors, walls and ceilings – emphasises cleanliness, its uneven textured surfaces creating subtle shadows as they catch the light. The strong presence of long, custom-made silver washbasins presents a new kind of restroom ritual, their curved and rounded structures embracing visitors' hands as they wash. The sensation of being saturated by the colour of light transforms all elements of the restroom experience into something extraordinary, leaving a powerful, lasting impression on the visitor.

Interview with Yohei Terui & Hiromu Yuyama

Both of you did not major in design from the beginning when you were students, which is a unique background. Please tell us about your backgrounds behind it.

Hiromu: In college, I was in the physics education department. My father was an architectural designer, but I never thought of design as a profession. When I decided to go to school, I was good at science and interested in teaching. I didn't study much while in school, though, and played rugby all four years. I really enjoyed my educational training and felt that the children liked me, but I felt that being a school teacher, a position in which people are evaluated, did not fit my way of life. When I thought back to what I genuinely liked, two things occurred to me: First, from the first time I was given my own room in elementary school, I had been playing with it, changing the layout once a month, which I really enjoyed. I couldn't change the size or shape of the room or windows, and the desks and chairs were the same, but I enjoyed realising that just by changing the arrangement, the atmosphere of the space could be very different. Another experience was in the early 2000s, when a fashion shopping site opened and I saw a number of imaginary store designs on the web. Although they were all computer-generated, they were realistic and original, and I was impressed by the possibilities of what could be done with space. After graduating from college, I decided to attend a school for interior and architectural design. There, I got so involved that I felt like a fish out of water. We were given a number of design assignments in specific settings, and we had to design a space from the conceptualisation stage and make a presentation. It was exciting to see how other students approached the same conditions and how the professor evaluated them, and it was like a competition among all my classmates all over again.

Yohei: I was a commerce major in college. Before college, I attended an integrated junior high and high school for boys in Yokohama, and I was really into skateboarding and surfing at that time. After school, I would go to Shonan area with my board on the side of my motorised bike. I think that is when I developed my sense of physical movement. I think I always placed importance on being in an environment where I could move quickly and agilely. At that time in the 90s, I was really into street culture and music. I also liked experiences and music that gave me a sense of floating. There was a sense of being suddenly released from gravity, which led to my taste in all things. When I entered college, I became more interested in the art field, but I also saw it as some special, separate world. In the meantime, I had the opportunity to participate in a lighting design event and developed a strong interest in space. There is an atmosphere in a space, and in a live music venue. For example, everyone reacts to the music and the entire space becomes one. Through such experiences, I thought it would be great if I could work in a way that people could share what I thought was good and deliver it to others. Later, my interest in space and lighting design grew stronger, and I moved to the United States to study interior design at a school in New York. I wanted to immerse myself in an environment with many different values, which was another reason why I chose the United States. And above all, I had a strong yearning for New York. In fact, it was a very stimulating environment where I had friendly competition with students from many different countries and departments. Since I had a language disadvantage, I think the first part of the program was a time for me to hone my expressions, especially those that were easy to understand. Then, from the second year, we moved on to more specialised spatial design, and I remember becoming absorbed in the architectural approach of the teachers, who were not decorative, but rather focused on the essence of the space.

Where did you choose to work once you entered the design field?

Hiromu: When I thought about starting work two years after I began to study design seriously, I realized that there were many designers in the world that I did not know and that there were as many ways of thinking as there were designers. I thought it would be good to be somewhere where there were many designers, so I approached several large organisational design firms. Then I was hired by one design firm called ILYA. When I actually joined the company organisation I found that each designer had a different sensibility, and different generations had various ways of thinking, and I was able to experience different ways of approaching design. Many of the projects were large-scale, such as designing the entire interior of an office building or hotel. But I come from a spatial experience of redecorating rooms, so the scale felt a little too far away. In my third year of work, a classmate from vocational school and I quit the company to try to start our own business, and we worked together for about a year, but since we didn't have much of a track record yet, the time passed by more through trial and error on what to do with the office than with the projects. I felt again that I wanted to be more seriously involved in design to the point where my body would be worn out. That is why I opened the door to Curiosity, a design firm. Curiosity's case studies had been featured in design media not only in Japan but also overseas, and each project left a strong impression on me.

Yohei: I was looking for a job in New York and sent my portfolio to several firms. I think the strength of the design was more important to me than the size of the firm. As a student, I interned at Gabellini Sheppard Associates. After graduation, I joined SHoP Architects. I went through competitions and other experiences for a while, but then in 2008 the big economic recession happened and restructuring storms occurred all over the world. It was a really tough time for everyone, including myself, and the atmosphere in New York City was heavy. I was very anxious about the future, especially as a newcomer to the workforce and a foreigner. After returning to Japan, I joined Curiosity. In the company, we were making perspective drawings using computer graphics and discussing design, and I remember feeling somewhat relieved because the process was the same as in an American office. And Gwenael Nicolas, the founder of Curiosity, had an approach that went beyond interiors, which I really enjoyed. He also thoroughly emphasised the importance of making the design strong. At first I thought I wanted to be independent someday, but the projects were always fascinating, the creative things were always happening around me in an exciting and stimulating environment and as a design student, I couldn't have asked for a better context. I ended up staying at Curiosity for about eight and a half years.

Why did the two of you decide to start your own firm independent of Curiosity?

Hiromu: I had been with Curiosity for about four years, and it was time for me to do something different. At the time, about 80% of Curiosity's projects were overseas, and so were the clients. And all of the projects were very attractive. I was enjoying working at a Japanese office, but also the idea of working for foreign company on overseas local projects, was quite interesting to me, too. At that time, Yohei asked me if I would like to start our own company together.

Yohei: The staff at Curiosity were all excellent people, and I was really surprised when I joined the firm. I still think the same now, but I believe through actual experience that it is the same everywhere in the world that a design firm that is famous in its time attracts great people who are in season at that time.

When I thought about bringing the firm together with someone else, I immediately thought about Hiromu. For example, there were a lot of experimental materials in the office at that time, and the staff would play with them, and each person's sense of style would come out. I sympathised with the way he expressed his originality there, not to mention the design quality. He often talks about 'new things,' and I thought his commitment to newness was amazing as a designer. I also think it was important for us to have a good fit in terms of 'quality behavior.' There is a range of 'quality' from elegant to vulgar, but when working together, I think it is most important to share where we set this line.

Hiromu: I was torn between what to do and what to do with the company, but from that time on, Yohei told me that he

It is very important what kind of feeling people get when they come to a place. It's about how the feelings move.

Hiromu Yuyama

wanted to create a company that had a future. I felt a great deal of sympathy for his fundamental thinking about what a company should be in the first place, rather than about what kind of design or work a company should do. I felt that Yohei had a broad perspective that looked at the root of various issues.

What was important to you when working as I IN?

Hiromu: We were groping for what kind of designer we wanted to be at first, but we had the idea of 'memorable design' from the beginning. We didn't know exactly what that was at first, but we gradually began to understand. It was only when we began to understand that we were able to confirm what had been there since the first bakery store we worked on.

Yohei: The expression 'refined' is also commonly used. Looking at the bakery store again now, we wonder if we were able to achieve the expression we were looking for. 'Why is that?' we wondered. Was it because of the obvious things like light and materials? We think that I IN's individuality will emerge when the individuality and newness of each of the artists is further fleshed out.

One project that was a turning point for us was the 'Warp Studio' office project that started at the end of our first year. The client had a very strong desire to create something new, and the word 'future' was repeatedly spoken and mentioned. He was especially willing to work with us to find a clear vision of the future. I believe that this project created the opportunity to be 'future-like' or 'future-oriented' in the design process.

Hiromu: In the 1990s, there were many futuristic expressions using new technologies. When we became independent, there seemed to be an atmosphere of going back and focusing on what was essential and how to brush up on the status quo, rather than a world that looked to the future. However, there seemed to be few opportunities to look to the future as designers. In our previous projects, we had a desire to create something new, but we felt that we were not communicating designs that were connected to the future. That is when we came across the keyword 'future,' but we thought that futuristic things are not the future. It gave me an opportunity to rethink what kind of future design we should be thinking about from now on.

The person in charge of 'Warp Studio' requested me to create a place to express large 8K images somewhere. What he was saying was that 8K had crossed the line from previous image technologies and was reaching a point where the barrier between reality and virtuality was breaking down. When we ourselves actually experienced 8K on a large screen, it was clear that this was indeed the case. Rather than technology being ahead of us, it really made us think about the relationship of how technology exists in the world we are in now, and we began to think about what new things we could do if we translated it into space through design.

Yohei: The word 'future' can be converted to 'new,' but 'new' is quite difficult to translate. What is new to me may not be new to others. But at the very least, we think that we should definitely create something new for ourselves. First of all, I would like to be able to say, 'I think this is new.' I think that is the most important thing for a designer.

Hiromu: The 'future' might also be paraphrased as 'the unknown.'

Yohei: When there are words like that, it motivates people to want to take a look. It is the same for the designers, the people who make the furniture and the client. Basically, we don't use the same design for the same project, and if possible, we would like to make all the furniture. It's a lot of work, but if we have to go through the trouble, that shows how much we want to do it.

Are there any other projects that were turning points for you?

Yohei: The next major change came with the arrival of a residency project. At first, we were asked to consult on some friend's houses, which led us to face the residential space. As our work on residences gradually increased, we were asked to work on a renovation housing project called 'THELIFE' from the branding stage. This was another opportunity to expand ourselves.

Hiromu: While 'newness' is absolutely our base, what we value equally is 'quality.' I believe that quality comes from the fact that there are definitely people there. It is very important what kind of feeling people get when they come to a place. It's about how the feelings move. I think it is very important that there is surprise and excitement at the first moment of the experience, and that there is something you can feel even if you stay there for another hour. That is quality. I don't think that just being new or high quality is enough to convey our unique design.

Yohei: We have also designed events, and I think we have become able to do this because we have worked in many different genres. Whether it is an office, a store or a house, it is new and something that no one has ever thought of before, yet it still feels good, and I think that is what makes us unique. I think the reason why we were approached by 'THELIFE' is because we live in an age where it is easier for clients to know what they like, and it is easier for them to choose the designers they like.

Hiromu: However, I still worry about the predictability of 'this is what you will get if you ask this designer to do it.' Being predictable is an advantage. If you can predict what kind of design you will get, it is easier to ask that designer to do the job. However, in order to do that, you need to keep producing similar output. For us, it is best if people think, 'I don't know what I can expect from these people, but I have high expectations.'

Yohei: And the third turning point is Blue Bottle Coffee Umeda Chayamachi Cafe. As you might know, Blue Bottle Coffee has a variety of designers involved in each project, each expressing their own ideas. As a designer, it is very interesting to see how each company expresses itself within the same limitations. Through this project, I feel that I was able to show I IN's unique expressions more clearly by being able to compare them with those of others. However, we will not repeat the same expressions, so if we receive a new project with the same conditions, we will propose a completely different approach from the previous one. This project was an opportunity for us to reexamine the meaning of our own existence and to communicate it more broadly to the outside world.

What do you pay attention to when communicating with clients?

Hiromu: Especially at the beginning, I try not to interrupt the client's words, but rather try to get a sense of who the client is, what he or she is thinking and how he or she wants the project to be done. I try to input not only keywords, but also information that cannot be put into form, such as wording, detailed nuances, etc. Even in the case of brainstorming discussions, I try not to give specific pictures, saying, 'Well, let's do this.' Even when there is a brainstorming discussion, we avoid giving concrete pictures of 'this is what it means' or 'let's do it this way then.' If you have a visual image before the design is created, you instill that image ahead of time. If this is the case, it becomes the base of the design, and it will not be oriented toward creating something new. So, as much as possible, our initial communication is based on words alone, without showing concrete shapes or colours. There are cases where images are shown, but I try to extract what is being said and what they are looking for.

Yohei: It's like we meet, talk naturally and breathe together. However, I may value speed, including response, in our interactions. Taking time to think about a proposal increases its value. Also, with time, most things are feasible; without time, they are impossible.

How long do you have to prepare your first presentation?

Yohei: We allow roughly one month from the first meeting to the presentation. Conversely, the primary value we have is in the first month. During that month, we prepare the materials for the presentation, study the basic plan and so on. The rest of the time is the control phase. In the presentation, we used to present only one plan, but recently we have been thinking that it would be good to have two plans alone. Sometimes the client wants to see more than one, and sometimes it means drawing out what we have. And in the end, the two may become better as one.

Hiromu: However, we don't unnecessarily produce many patterns; whether it is one or two, it is important to see how far we can refine them in a limited amount of time. Of course, in a design study, we start from the path of having several ideas at first. As you refine from there, the patterns naturally converge. As a result, when I come up with several ideas, I am often asked, 'Which do you recommend?' and it turns out that both are recommended ideas.

Does it take you a while to come up with a plan that says, 'Let's go with this'?

Hiromu: There is something in the beginning that says, 'This must be what it means this time.' It doesn't take long to get to that point. But then we take it one step further by breaking it down. This is where new things emerge, but it is very difficult to break them down. In the first stage, it may depend on the person, but it seems to come out as a landscape of 'this kind of space,' somehow. If you try to share it between two people, you end up looking for an image to share, as I mentioned earlier. It

I think it's good to have unpredictable things happen and come up with new ideas, so I don't make too many decisions, but rather concentrate and work slowly for a month while having the capacity to accept unpredictable things.

Yohei Terui

is difficult to do so, because then it could lose its freshness. I was listening to an interview a musician gave the other day, and I could relate. For that musician, the music in its purest state of imagination, with no lyrics, just sound, was the purest. He said that the lyrics are added to the song to force it to fit.

Yohei: I think everything we see is stocked in our mind. Something that caught my attention is probably in a corner of my mind. And when I think about a project for a presentation, it's like I've been given a subject. For example, when designing a sushi restaurant, while my mind is occupied with the sushi restaurant, the things in my head are stimulated. I think it is the structure of the brain that subconsciously connects with what it sees, and something is created. So, during the month, I raise my mind and concentrate. At first, I always draw sketches by hand, and then I create the perspective in CG. Sometimes I make a little mistake and things change, which is quite interesting. Sometimes, unexpected colors are added and unexpected effects are produced. I think it's good to have unpredictable things happen and come up with new ideas, so I don't make too many decisions, but rather concentrate and work slowly for a month while having the capacity to accept unpredictable things.

Also, I always try to be stimulated on a regular basis. I try to leave something that I think is good, even if it is just a view. It is difficult to do so when I am busy, but if I couldn't do that, it would be difficult to keep doing this job. I try to look at various genres of things other than design, and I want to broaden my horizons as much as possible. Omotesando, where our office is located, is lined with many flagship stores of high-end brands, but the recent messages from such brands are often young and fresh. I think the stimulation we receive from the city is linked to our own activities.

How do you split roles between the two of you?

Yohei: There are no specific roles that are separate, but there are responsibilities for each project. How they are divided is not decided in particular; sometimes the person wants to be in charge, and sometimes it is just the right time of year. This stance has not changed since we started the company.

Hiromu: Good thing about having two people is that they have different perspectives. When you are in charge of a project, basically the person in charge will be the main communicator with the client and will look at every detail. Through this process, the design gets deeper and more polished. The other person, on the other hand, looks at the project objectively in a sense, maintaining a fresh perspective, such as what a person coming to a place for the first time would feel or think. Both perspectives are necessary, and I imagine that the position switches depending on which person is in charge of each project.

Yohei: I would like that to be the same no matter how many I INs there are. In the end, however, we should put out what we have done as individuals. We have two representatives now, but no matter how many people we have, whether three or four, we will put out what we have done. Even if the number of members increases, I would like to make this a company where everyone can grow and develop through the mutual development of each other's strengths and individuality. However, it is important to ensure our design. Our goal is to create a team with a strong group of players, not just a bunch of designers, so we place importance not only on individual training but also on unity as a company. No matter who is in charge of the design, it will be I IN's design. I believe that by doing so, our name will remain more as a company than as individuals.

More than anything else, I think it is more enjoyable for me to be in a place where there are many different designers. I am always wondering what kind of design he will do this time, or what I will do this time, and we are both stimulating each other to grow and update the company's creativity.

Is there anything you pay attention to in the way you carry out your projects?

Hiromu: There is something to be said for putting something somewhere in a project that you are not sure if you can do. If we didn't do that, we wouldn't be able to create a fresh design.

Yohei: During a presentation, we are asked, 'Have you ever done this before?' We are afraid to answer, 'No, we have not,' when asked. But I think such a challenge would be a motivation for everyone involved.

Hiromu: It is very important to create an atmosphere where people can enjoy the work together. It is also significant to give the client an attractive presentation that makes them want to see the project, and it is also important to give many ideas of what could be done in the course of conversation so that the client feels that the project will be completed. No matter how much we think about it, the final space will not be created without the client who gives us the go-ahead, and without the contractors and manufacturers who collaborate with us. We take care in our communication with these people so that we can enjoy the project as it progresses.

Yohei: Projects take a long time, and there are ups and downs in the process. At the time of the initial proposal, you get excited and say, 'Great.' Then, when things settle down a bit and realistic costs come into view, the momentum drops off dramatically. Then, as the parties involved discuss the project, there is a moment when they realize that it can be done, and from that moment on, everyone's power suddenly rises to the top and construction begins. Feeling this power and upward momentum is one of the best parts of the job.

Hiromu: The more we can make that vector upward, the better the final product will be. It is a series of various choices, and I feel it is a paper-thin difference.

What would you like to do in the future?

Hiromu: We would like to design a wide range of areas based on the design of space. I would like to go beyond walls and move from interiors to exteriors, from hand-held objects such as furniture and products to the scale of monuments and plazas, and I would like to consistently design various places by considering them as spaces.

In that sense, I am also interested in designing unreal spaces. Until now, people who designed real and unreal spaces were divided, and their usage was also different. However, as gadgets such as goggles and the expression of content evolve further, designers and their uses will be integrated, and it would be interesting to design realistic unrealistic spaces as a designer of realistic spaces.

All of this is also because I want more people to experience

I IN design. What I would like to do for this purpose is to design products that are easy to pick up, to design plazas where many people can gather and to design virtual spaces that can be experienced beyond physical distance.

Yohei: I IN started in 2018 and this year will be 6 years. I would like to achieve more results so that I IN's name can be properly recognised overseas. There are many Japanese architects whose names are recognised worldwide, but there are not many interior designers yet. The reason why I want to work out of our comfort zone is because we can express ourselves in a slightly different vector than usual, and we can stimulate each other by meeting various creative people. And we believe that this experience will lead us to expand the possibilities of our designs.

As I mentioned earlier, our ultimate goal is to keep updating our creativity, so I believe that expressing ourselves with high dimensionality under various circumstances will lead to our own evolution.

In general, Asian designers have a strong impression of simplicity in design, but there are times when more texture, massiveness and glamour are demanded, especially in luxury design, by global standards. We believe that this is where the next level of quality that can be accepted globally lies. Our goal is to reach and compete at that level first. We believe that interior design, which is related to food, clothing and housing, has a strong influence on society and can build an affluent lifestyle. I hope to continue to move forward with the goal of creating a bright future.

BLUE BOTTLE COFFEE UMEDA CHAYAMACHI CAFÉ

CAFÉ
OSAKA, JAPAN (2021)

As this was the first Blue Bottle Coffee shop to be opened in this region, the interior design was crucial in delivering the brand's message and conveying a straightforward story to customers. The iconic blue logo suddenly appears in the cityscape, and the joy of discovering the familiar hue of the brand is expressed using various lights and materials. Historically, the location of Chayamachi has a unique Japanese tea culture, where people gather and share time. This sense of unity is interpreted modernly throughout the whole café. On the first floor, the customer is surrounded by the essence of warm wood, a big drip station filled with bright, welcoming light and a stage-like space where the barista making coffee stands out the most. The counter is made of polished stainless steel hairline and shows a dignified presence. The surface reflects the scenery of the space, softening the boundary between the barista and customers. The unique blue glass throughout the store expresses the brand's iconic character with its unique transparency. The product is placed there to directly convey the brand's message. By the staircase area, a glass chandelier hung from the ceiling spreads throughout the atrium. Made by an Osaka-based glass artist, coffee-coloured spherical glass glass gently welcomes guests. Customers can feel the flow of an impressive view of light and colour with the three-dimensional spatial experience of the stairs. A particular area is located in the centre of the second floor, mainly surrounded by white-coloured materials, stimulating the visitors' five senses. By spending time here while bathing in the images and sounds that 'fall' from the ceiling, guests create a memorable experience that can change the impression of time and stimulate their senses. Created in collaboration with Panoramatiks, pictures and music allow customers to fully reset themselves. The bench, made out of a special material, has a mechanism only the person sitting upon it can encounter through a sensory experience.

PINOCCHIO

BAKERY
YOKOHAMA, JAPAN (2019)

A bakery located at the landmark Matsubara shopping street in Japan's Yokohama city, Kanagawa prefecture. A solid wood table, installed at the centre of the store with a strong presence, creates an immediate and unforgettable impression. It is a strong focus point that presents the bread and pastries in an intuitively natural setting. The unique irregularity and texture of the wood, achieved over time, create a high-quality expression of the space. Another distinctive feature of the store is its wide street-facing façade. By installing a long table in the middle of the bakery, we created a simultaneously external and internal form that was easily visible and recognisable from the street. Soft façade lighting further emphasises the flow of the seasons and the shift of day into night. This is Pinocchio's second store, a bakery in front of Oguchi Station in Yokohama, Kanagawa Prefecture. The façade, expressed by the colour of baked bread, provides a solid presence to the station square. Vivid gradients and soft textures that express the quality and colour of the bread are spread both inside and outside the store. The interior space, where all elements are kept to a minimum and iconic wood surrounds the space, offers a sense of intimacy for the visitors. An emblematic appearance that can be recognised immediately from a distance and a space with a soft impression through the materials and light allows the bread to stand out, creating a new bakery image.

WARP STUDIO

OFFICE
TOKYO, JAPAN (2019)

The office for Mitsui Fudosan is a new type of space designed by I IN and used by company members for various independent projects. A different office style was required to create a new business for the well-known Japanese company. The space had to differ from the typical office space, where the usual atmosphere would be for people to work at their desks. The point was to create an office where people could relax and spend their free time. In essence, the feeling of being in one's own house was taken into inspiration and applied to all common spaces, such as living and dining environments. To create a place where people can feel the future, technology that embraces everyday life has been used to express newness. A high-resolution screen with high-output images flowing in the centre of the office emits colour-lit pictures throughout the whole space. By blurring the boundaries between the image and the reality, I IN aimed for an expression symbolising the actual future. In contrast to the open space, the meeting room, surrounded by a plastered curved wall with soft shading, is much quieter, and the design reflects its calmness. Using characteristic colour gradation through the glass, slightly coloured light flows into the room. By rebuilding light, shape, materials and how people spend their time at work, the whole office becomes a comfortable space, presenting a new view of the future.

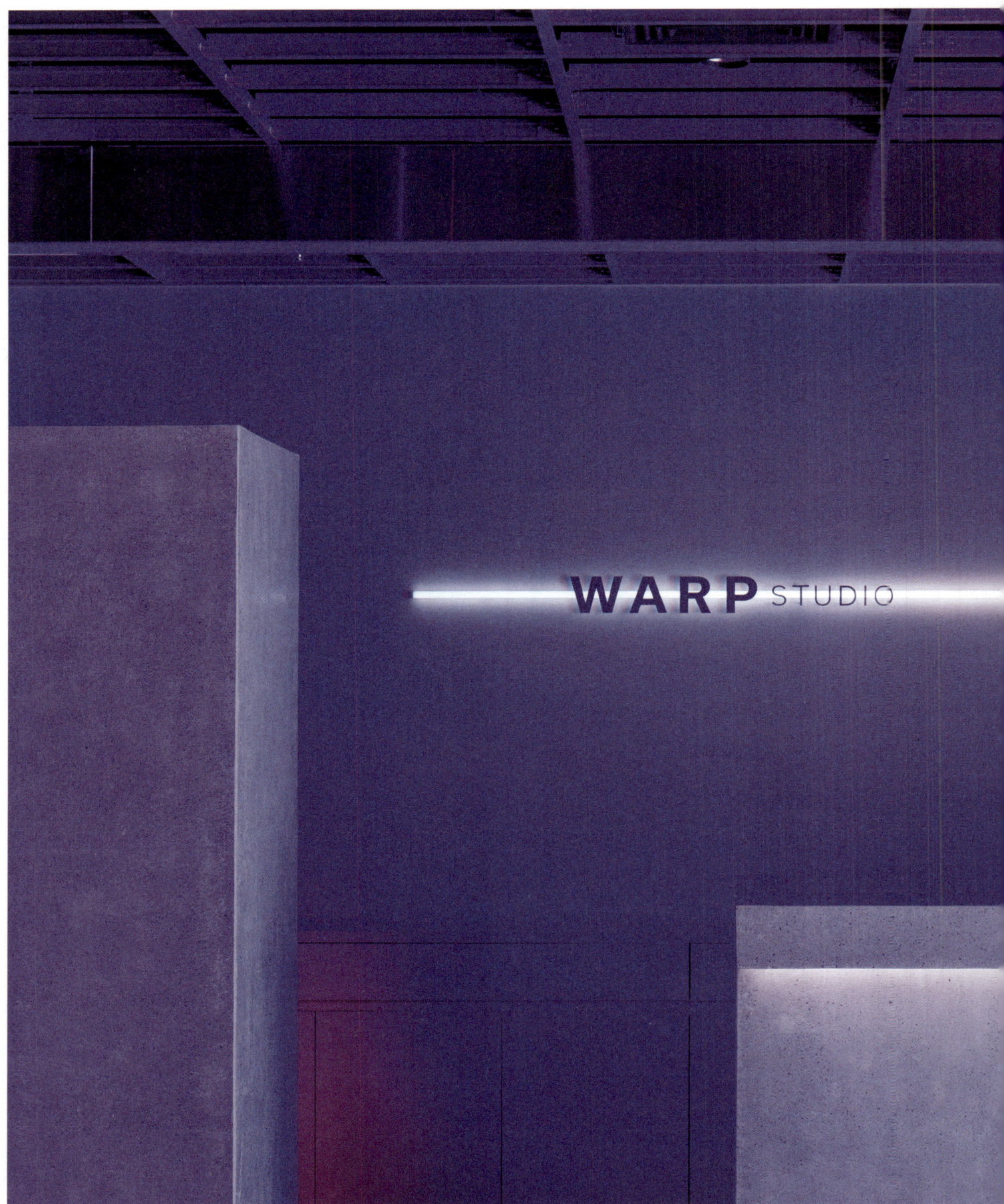

SHISEIDO
FUTURE SOLUTION LX

RETAIL
SHANGHAI, CHINA (2020)

This is Shiseido's skincare brand's first flagship store, Future Solution LX. By paying attention to the soft light and dynamism created by the smooth shapes and the power of Japanese materials, which is also the essence of the brand, I IN expressed the delicate charm that makes us feel the mysterious power of nature and the atmosphere of Japan. The façade with an organic form allows the customer to feel the dynamic energy of nature, with its walls finished in plaster with fine irregularities and gently inviting people in like a vessel. The iridescent light, which is the product colour of Future Solution LX, gently flows on the central screen and illuminates the entire store. It also creates a sparkle with the prism of the textured glass. In the salon space for consultations, in various places, customers can spend a rich time surrounded by high-quality materials from Japan, such as the stone top produced in the Japanese mountains of Miyagi prefecture or cushions made of Nishijin woven fabric from Kyoto. The private room where customers can have a private beauty experience is filled with material, creating an iridescent colour from a reaction with the light. The three-dimensional chandelier made out of fabric and suspended from the ceiling creates the sensation of entering into a smooth jade-colour light. The timeless expressions have been realised by introducing new characters to modern technology and materials passed down in Japan for a long time.

GOODLIFE

OFFICE
TOKYO, JAPAN (2022)

The Goodlife Office is a space designed for the headquarters of Goodlife, a venture company that is revolutionising the real estate business with AI. Goodlife is a dynamic company combining its progressive approach to services with the high trust essential to the real estate industry. Our aim was to create a space that expressed the quality of a company dedicated to such values. The Goodlife logo at the entrance is a sculptural work lit in red, blue and green, the company's corporate colours. Indirect lighting emanates from within, emphasising the logo's form, and softly radiates outwards. Beyond the entrance lies an open-plan lounge, an ambient space for employees and guests to mingle, relax and converse. Bespoke furniture and unique long pendant lamps are arranged to echo the monochrome striations of the space's carpeting. Amplified by a wall mirror, these flowing lines accentuate perspective in a space through which time seems to visually accelerate. As if frozen in this temporal dimension, a bold granite counter becomes the focal point of the lounge. A powerful presence, its monumental form highlights the scale and quality of the stone used. Directly above, three strips of coloured light infuse the area with the corporate red, green and blue, their hues subtly blending into and influencing each other. The visual experience of being immersed in light, shadows and colour leaves all visitors with vivid memories. This design proposes a new office style built from the relationships between light, colour and materials for a company renowned for its new and innovative business ideas.

LULLA HOUSE

RESIDENCE
KAMAKURA, JAPAN (2024)

Lulla House is a weekend house that reflects a client's lifestyle who has launched a fashion brand. It serves as both the owner's residence and the brand's home. The layout, materials, furniture and details exude elegance, uniqueness, majesty, softness and suggestiveness. For this house, the design aim was to depict the client's dignified personality through the space itself. Surrounded by the ocean, the beach and the sky, the location is so overwhelming that you feel like you are part of the environment. Looking out of the window, all elements of the exterior scene are captured within the frame: Waves flowing, birds drifting in the wind, people playing on the beach, a distant coastline with mountains faintly visible and the sun setting between the sea and the sky. The large windows on the west side were designed with a sense of scale, making it feel as if one could physically immerse oneself in the outside world. In the centre of the space, a newly installed spiral staircase awaits visitors, while lights on the walls guide and invite people to each space like a lantern. The wooden pieces in the house were brushed to give an impression of lifelike texture. The human sensibilities emanate from the floors and walls, which were meticulously finished by hand on-site, enriching the space with a touch of life and elegance. The third floor of Lulla House has a unique layout. Going up the stairs, one would be greeted by an open closet strategically placed at the house's core – a bright and airy space – to symbolise the centrality of dressing in one's lifestyle. The open bathroom, which gives one a sense of unity with the ocean, occupies nearly half of the third floor. From the shower room and vanity counter to the bathtub, spaces for interacting with water are seamlessly connected. The pink tiles are assembled with yellow grout as an accent, making the space appear fashionably playful, echoing the process of working with cloth and thread. All the furniture was designed with the client's individual character in mind. A dignified appearance, graceful figure and pure ideas, all of which harmonise beautifully together under one roof.

AFTERWORD

Characterising the work of I IN is much like peeling the layers of an onion. The eye is immediately drawn to spaces that impress with their simplicity – there is no excess of materials, no unnecessary details and no gimmicky objects present.

However, these spaces are far from cold or impersonal. Rounded structures and curved corners instantly make visitors feel at ease. Fluid lines are soothing to the eye. Warm colours, often derived from natural materials, welcome people and invite them to linger. The colour gradient in I IN's oeuvre deserves special mention. By enriching surfaces, gradients suggest the radiant presence of concealed light sources, adding depth to the space.

Peeling back another layer reveals what could be termed I IN's secret ingredient: The studio's use of light. Soft, often natural, lighting shapes space and enhances the spatial experience. In the hands of I IN's founders, Yohei Terui and Hiromu Yuyama, light becomes a tool to add drama and depth to rooms. The designers also use light to highlight merchandise. But above all, lighting imparts a sense of calm and sensuality to many of I IN's projects. The green and yellow ambience in the public toilets of the Shin-Marunouchi Building not only subtly blurs gender boundaries but also immerses visitors in a physical experience where intimacy and sensuality intersect with cleanliness. At the heart of the Blue Bottle Coffee shop in Osaka, a glass-enclosed room invites coffee enthusiasts to rest while blue light from an artificial skylight soothes their senses. Consider the glowing red entrance of the Ya-man flagship store, a sign of the facial gym experience clients will encounter inside.

The interiors by I IN may appear simple, but they require a deep understanding of aesthetics, an eye for detail and a healthy dose of empathy. Whether for retail environments, residences or workplaces, the designers at I IN create exquisitely refined solutions for today's complex problems while hinting at the future. Their approach to spatial design could be labelled as New Luxury. Marble, gold and opulence are the hallmarks of the old luxury world. New Luxury is characterised by careful attention, absolute reduction and gentle refinement, resulting in spaces that promote wellbeing. This is the gift that I IN offers us.

Robert Thiemann

PROJECT INFORMATION

CARTIER GUEST LOUNGE

CLIENT
Richemont Japan

CONSTRUCTION
Takashimaya Space Create

LIGHTING DESIGN
hmmm

FURNITURE PRODUCTION
Time & Style

PHOTOGRAPHY
Tomooki Kengaku

POKÉMON CENTER OKINAWA

CLIENT
The Pokémon Company

CONSTRUCTION
e-store planning

LIGHTING DESIGN
hmmm

MOVIE
WOW

PHOTOGRAPHY
Tomooki Kengaku

©2022 Pokémon.
©1995-2022 Nintendo/Creatures Inc./
GAME FREAK inc.

YA-MAN

CLIENT
YA-MAN

CONSTRUCTION
Takashimaya Space Create

LIGHTING DESIGN
hmmm

PHOTOGRAPHY
Tomooki Kengaku

THELIFE

CLIENT
GOODLIFE

CONSTRUCTION
JPDH

LIGHTING DESIGN
USHIO LIGHTING

ART WORKS
A Lighthouse called Kanata

PHOTOGRAPHY
Norihito Yamauchi

CARTIER JAPAN OFFICE

CLIENT
Richemont Japan

CONSTRUCTION
Takashimaya Space Create

LIGHTING DESIGN
hmmm

FURNITURE PRODUCTION
Time & Style

PHOTOGRAPHY
Tomooki Kengaku

MASTERMIND

CLIENT
mastermind JAPAN

CONSTRUCTION
Interior Murakami

LIGHTING DESIGN
LIGHT CUBE

PHOTOGRAPHY
Norihito Yamauchi

MARUNOUCHI HOUSE TOILET

CLIENT
MITSUBISHI ESTATE

DESIGN COLLABORATION
MITSUBISHI JISHO DESIGN

PROJECT MANAGEMENT
MITSUBISHI JISHO PROPERTY MANAGEMENT

CONSTRUCTION
NOMURA

LIGHTING DESIGN
hmmm

PHOTOGRAPHY
Tomooki Kengaku

BLUE BOTTLE COFFEE UMEDA CHAYAMACHI CAFÉ

CLIENT
Blue Bottle Coffee Japan

CONSTRUCTION
TANK, Atelier Loöwe

LIGHTING DESIGN
Y LIGHTS

DIGITAL ART
Panoramatiks

PHOTOGRAPHY
Tomooki Kengaku

PINOCCHIO

CLIENT
Yokohama shokusan

CONSTRUCTION
Legoretta

LIGHTING DESIGN
I IN

PHOTOGRAPHY
Satoshi Shigeta
Tomooki Kengaku

WARP STUDIO

CLIENT
Mitsui Fudosan

PROJECT MANAGEMENT
Cosmos More

CONSTRUCTION
MITSUI Designtec

LIGHTING DESIGN
LIGHT CUBE

PHOTOGRAPHY
Tomooki Kengaku

SHISEIDO FUTURE SOLUTION LX

CLIENT
SHISEIDO

CONSTRUCTION
DC International

LIGHTING DESIGN
LIGHT CUBE /
KOIZUMI LIGHTING

MOVIE
WOW

PHOTOGRAPHY
Wu Qingshan

GOODLIFE

CLIENT
GOODLIFE

CONSTRUCTION
REM

LIGHTING DESIGN
DN LIGHTING

PHOTOGRAPHY
Norihito Yamauchi

LULLA HOUSE

CLIENT
LEMONADE

CONSTRUCTION
TANK

FURNITURE PRODUCTION
Time & Style

LIGHTING DESIGN
hmmm

PHOTOGRAPHY
Tomooki Kengaku

SPECIAL THANKS

Aki Komiya
Akihiro Yamada
Akiko Satake
Akio Kyusai
Akira Karashima
Akira Ota
Akira Shibasaki
Ami Taniguchi
Anouk Haegens
Ariel Raphael Asken
Asami Harada
Ashitako Arakawa
Atsushi Omae
Ayumi Tatematsu
Azusa Yamato
Ben Duncan
Cajsa Carlson
Cary Cheng
Chinatsu Kaneko
Chris Lee
Chris Leong
Christopher Ax
Dai Kurihara
Daichi Yamato
Daizy Ho
Daven Wu
David Gao
David Guarino
DIN Films
Eiji Hiraide
Eiji Yoshida
Eiko Idaira
Eriko Kobayashi
Filiz Altan
Floor Kuitert
François-Luc Giraldeau
Gaku Masui
Go Hagiwara
Go Tashiro
Gordon Woo
Gorou Yamamura
Gwenael Nicolas
Hajime Kimura
Hajime Utoyama
Haruna Furuya
Helene Oberman
Hideharu Igarashi
Hikaru Mugita
Hiroaki Miyagawa
Hironari Oyamada

Hiroshi Kimura
Hiroshi Sugihara
Hiroshi Takahashi
Hiroshi Watanabe
Hirotaka Yamamoto
Hisaaki Hirawata
Hitomi Yuyama
Hitoshi Motomura
Isao Sato
Jiro Koga
Jo Gwon
Johnny Sidhu
Jun Kato
Junpei Deguchi
Kaoru Ikeda
Katsuji Isohara
Katsuyuki Haruki
Kayoko Terui
Kazuhiro Onuma
Kazuhiro Sugai
Kazuho Takahashi
Kazuki Kakei
Kazuya Takamori
Keiji Ashizawa
Keisuke Hori
Keisuke Kokubo
Keisuke Nakamori
Kenichi Shiota
Kenichiro Watanabe
Kensuke Kasai
Kento Shimohira
Kiichi Kondo
Kimiyo Yamazaki
Ko Arimura
Kohei Osako
Koji Kodama
Koji Yamamoto
Kosuke Kawai
Kosuke Ohno
Kota Endo
Kousuke Kushioka
Kyoka Shimada
Lisa Marchesi
Makiko Busato
Makiko Inoue
Makoto Horiike
Makoto Uehara
Makoto Yamaguchi
Marina Suzuki
Marina Terui

Marlous Willems
Masaaki Takahashi
Masafumi Tashiro
Masahiro Furukawa
Masahiro Oie
Masahiro Tanaka
Masahiro Yoshioka
Masanori Igarashi
Masanori Imada
Masanori Kobayashi
Masaru Mogaki
Masashi Kasai
Masashi Nakano
Masashi Ota
Masashi Tsujimura
Masato Kure
Masayuki Murakami
Megumi Yoshida
Miki Shinde
Miki Tamura
Minami Yuyama
Mio Yamada
Mira Huussen
Misako Fujimoto
Mizuki Matsuura
Momoka Okuda
Motoshi Horii
Nao Takekoshi
Naoko Endo
Naoto Oguri
Naritake Fukumoto
Narumi Sato
Niki Wu
Nobuyoshi Hine
Nono Kito
Noor Al Qayem
Norifumi Yoshida
Norihito Yamauchi
Orie Takashige
Paul Chan
Reiji Yamakura
Reiko Miyamoto
Reiko Sudo
Rikiya Uekusa
Risa Miyata
Robert Thiemann
Ryo Ito
Ryo Takahashi
Ryo Yoshimura
Ryo Yuyama

Ryoko Sakata
Ryota Kamijo
Saki Igawa
Sakiko Tsurusawa
Sarasa Sekizuka
Satoshi Shigeta
Seigo Okazaki
Seiji Oguri
Shiho Mizuno
Shinsuke Sugino
Shintaro Hayama
Shintaro Monden
Shinya Inobe
Shiyori Masuda
Sho Komaya
Shogo Terui
Shota Toda
Shuhei Oya
Shuhei Yamane
Shuichi Arai
Shun Nagasaka
Sojiro Inoue
Stephane Masquet
Taisuke Hattori
Takahiro Saito
Takao Endo
Takashi Matsumura
Takashi Saito
Takashi Yamasaki
Takasuke Yamada
Takayuki Masuyama
Takehiro Okamoto
Takeshi Jingi
Takuma Nakaji
Takumi Iwata
Taro Nakamura
Tatsuji Yoshikawa
Tetsu Miyake
Tetsushi Kotani
Theodore Gen Knipfing
Tohru Yonekura
Tom Yamamoto
Tomo Akabane
Tomo Kawaharada
Tomoaki Hamada
Tomohiro Watabe
Tomoki Matsumoto
Tomomi Narita
Tomomi Sato
Tomooki Kengaku

Toru Kanyama
Toru Takeda
Toshihiko Shiomitsu
Toshihiko Yoshino
Toshihiro Kawasaki
Toshikazu Morita
Toshiki Kiriyama
Toshiro Takahashi
Toshitaka Tanaka
Tsutomu Ouchi
Utako Sugiyama
Wahei Aoyama
Wataru Kirisawa
Wataru Takahashi
Wu Qingshan
Xu Jun
Yamato Watanabe
Yasuhiko Teramoto
Yasuhiro Aihara
Yasuhiro Iinuma
Yasuki Yuyama
Yasuo Ishihara
Yasushi Yoshida
Yayoi Kubota
Yoichi Koura
Yoichi Magishi
Yoichiro Tamada
Yoko Fujitsuka
Yoriko Takahashi
Yoshihide Murakami
Yoshihisa Kawakita
Yoshiko Sakurai
Yu Furukawa
Yuichi Minagwa
Yuichi Murakami
Yuka Hasegawa
Yuka Kotani
Yuki Matsumoto
Yuki Shibata
Yukio Miyamori
Yumiko Mizutani
Yurie Isono Duncan
Yusuke Watanabe
Yuta Hikima
Yutaka Sasaki
Zi Min Ting

I IN

Founded in 2018, I IN Inc. is an internationally acclaimed Tokyo-based design firm. I IN pursues the world of modern luxury within a wide range of spatial design fields, including retail, restaurants, offices, residences and installations. The design process begins by delving into clients' mindsets and understanding their core values to identify intrinsic elements of their individuality. Communicating with clients and collaborators contributes to interiors that bring new brilliance and experiential values to light, colour, materials and gravity. In reawakening the senses to these universal and intangible design elements, I IN Inc. creates inspired spaces that evoke a new vision of richness for the world of the future – one grounded in the sublime beauty of its interiors.

I IN INTERIORS

PUBLISHER
Frame

MANAGING EDITOR
François-Luc Giraldeau

EDITORIAL ASSISTANT
Noor Al Qayem

TEXTS
FOREWORD by Noor Al Qayem and François-Luc Giraldeau
INTRODUCTION by Daven Wu
INTERVIEW by Jun Kato
AFTERWORD by Robert Thiemann

TEXT EDITOR
Frame and
Mio Yamada

GRAPHIC DESIGN
Norifumi Yoshida

PRINTING
IPP

TRADE DISTRIBUTION USA AND CANADA
ACC Art Books
6 West 18th Street
Suite 4BNYC
NY 10011E
ussales@accartbooks.com
T +1 212 645 1111
F +1 716 242 4811
Books are billed and shipped by The National Book Network

TRADE DISTRIBUTION BENELUX
Frame Publishers
Zeeburgerkade 1198
1019 VK Amsterdam
the Netherlands
distribution@frameweb.com
frameweb.com

TRADE DISTRIBUTION REST OF WORLD
Thames & Hudson Ltd
181A High HolbornLondon WC1V 7QX
United Kingdom
T +44 20 7845 5000
F +44 20 7845 5050

ISBN: 978-94-93211-63-4

© 2025 Frame Publishers, Amsterdam, 2025

All rights reserved. No part of this publication may be reproduced or transmitted in any form or by any means, electronic or mechanical, or any storage and retrieval system, without permission in writing from the publisher. Whilst every effort has been made to ensure accuracy, Frame Publishers does not under any circumstances accept responsibility for errors or omissions. Any mistakes or inaccuracies will be corrected in case of subsequent editions upon notification to the publisher.

The Koninklijke Bibliotheek lists this publication in the Nederlandse Bibliografie: detailed bibliographic information is available on the internet at http://picarta.pica.nl

Printed on acid-free paper produced from chlorine-free pulp. TCF
Printed in Poland

10 9 8 7 6 5 4 3 2 1